The Distance Learning Activity Book For Parents Just Barely Holding On To Their Last Shred Of Sanity

by Courtney Henning Novak
*A Mom Just Barely Holding
On To Her Last Shred of Sanity*

This is a very serious page. It is the Copyright Page. Let me tell you about copyright law. IT IS BORING. During my second year of law school, I signed up for Copyright Law, thinking that since I like books and movies, I would naturally love learning about copyright. WRONG. I took some painfully dull classes during my law school career, but Copyright Law was by far the worst of the lot.

Law school was actually not that bad. Now being a lawyer - *that* was brutal. Oy vey, I was never meant to be a lawyer. But since I spent good money to go to law school, I figured I'd better give the whole lawyer thing an honest try and thus spent a good eight years of my life letting the law crush my soul. So now you know that about me, and look, we are only on the Copyright Page.

The Copyright Page is such a scam, isn't it? You pay good money for a book and right away, you get a page that is blank except for some boring crap about the copyright. Yet I love you already, and I'm in a generous mood, and the kids are watching some questionable videos on YouTube, so I thought I'd give you some bang for your buck.

You know what this Copyright Page needs? A scuba diver and a taco.

Look! The Copyright! I nearly forgot. That would have been embarrassing.

to Nathan

&

Pippa and Julian

&

Netflix,
YouTube,
my children's tablets,
the DVR and
any other device
that entertains my kids
when I just can't deal
with this abomination
anymore. Which is
very, very often.

Table of Contents

These bears have nothing to do with the Table of Contents or any part of this book, for that matter, but it seemed a shame to let so much space go to waste.

How To Use This Book

There is no single right way to use this book. There are, however, a few wrong ways to use this book, so let's get those out of the way first.

Ways To NOT Use This Book:
1. As a present for your child's teacher or principal.
2. As a flotation device in the event of a water landing.

Everyone understand? Good. Let's move on.

Ways To Use This Book
1. Turn the page to the first activity. Do the first activity. Then proceed to the next activity, and so on, until you have completed the book.
2. Open the book to a random page and start there.
3. Make paper airplanes.
4. Give this book to a friend without young children and tell them to read it upside down while standing on a bed of nails and listening to heavy metal. Tell them that is what distance learning is like. Then they might begin to understand why we have that haunted desperate look in our eyes.
5. Carry the book with you everywhere, like a security blanket, and clutch it when you feel like your spirit is about to break.
6. Scream at the book when you need an outlet for your rage. Don't worry. It's a book. It won't mind (much).
7. Use it as a cover for the book you are secretly reading about how to hide your assets before divorcing your spouse.

Godspeed.

Distance Learning Merit Badges!

I love merit badges! I would like to earn merit badges for EVERYTHING. Distance learning would be so much more tolerable if we could all earn some bitching badges. Alas, the school districts are yet to get on board with this scheme. Let's all petition our school boards to issue merit badges to parents. In the meantime, at least we have this activity book. Color in the badges you have earned. No cheating! *I am watching you and I will know if you color in a badge before it has been properly earned.*

Broke Internet to Play
Hooky From School

Gossiped With Other Parents
About Super Annoying Kid

It's *Lord of the Flies* here,
who stole the conch?

Brain at capacity. Announced
shutdown of its own.

Fantasized about being
exiled to desert island

Swore would never again
grumble about packing school lunch

Realized this is actually hell

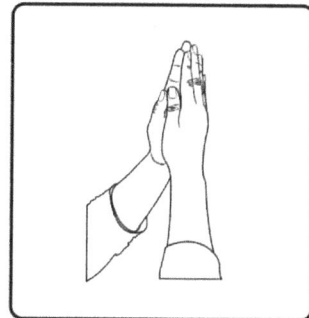

Satan

Bargained With
Higher Power

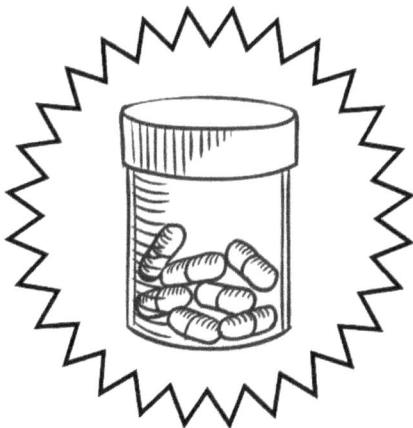

Increased or started prescription for
anti-depressants and anxiety meds

Ate entire cake,
still hated everything

Convinced trapped in
new surreal sequel
to *Groundhog Day*

Bawled Uncontrollably

Checked neighborhood for zombies
because that is only logical explanation

Considered joining dark
side of the Force

Spilled beverage
on schoolwork

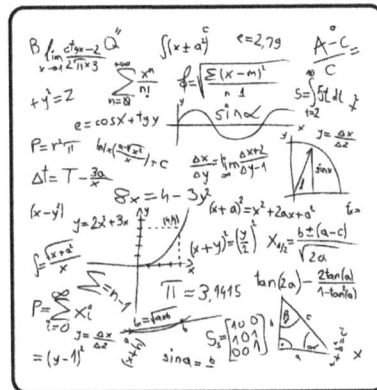

Cursed Math

Agitated parents, encouraged
mutiny and revolt

Abandoned hope,
succumbed to despair

Haunted by suspicion
this will never end

Literally out of fucks

Forgot to shower,
but who will ever know?

Beware my wrath,
all mortals shall cower &
tremble in my presence

Yes, You Absolutely Do Need A Distance Learning Nickname

Distance learning sucks. It drains parents of their life force and leaves them feeling feeble, forlorn and utterly devoid of laughter and joy. But you know what would return a little oomph to your soul? An epic nickname. The next time you are writing an epistle to the principal or talking about yourself in the third person, don't use the name your parents gave you. I'm sure they meant well, but names like "Courtney" and "Nathan" just don't inspire confidence during these dark times. Enter: the distance learning nickname.

A well-crafted distance learning nickname will give you a boost of confidence and add a little sparkle to your step. It will also force Your Child's Educational Authorities to take you more seriously. Every parent subjected to distance learning needs a wicked moniker.

But wait! You can't just *give* yourself a nickname. That violates Clause 17(a)(iii) of the International Uniform Code For The Regulation of Nicknomenclature, *One cannot both be the nicknamee and the nicknamor.* Translation: you cannot ask your friends to call you Zeus. (And yes, I know a guy who asked his friends to call him Zeus.) (He was a jackass.) (I'm sure he's a decent guy now.)

Fear not, broken and shattered readers! I have devised an activity that will help you determine your own snazzy distance learning nickname to strike fear into the hearts of all who read your Letters to the Editors and impress the parents at your child's school. But don't stop there! Give nicknames to all your friends and mortal enemies, and experience a flicker of something that resembles joy during the distance learning horror show. Remember joy? Yeah, me neither.

Step One: What is your birth month?

January:	Admiral	July:	Archangel
February:	Right Honorable	August:	Chef
March:	Darth	September:	Detective
April:	Doctor	October:	Warden
May:	President	November:	Uncle/Aunt
June:	Baron/Baroness	December:	Duke/Duchess

Step Two: What is your favorite color?

Red:	Red Velvet Cake	Plaid:	Footstool
Blue:	Bagel	Purple:	Velvet
Green:	Wombat	Rainbow:	Glitter
Orange:	Centaur	Teal:	Raisin Bread
Yellow:	Dodecahedron	Maroon:	Barm
Pink:	Marshmallow	Lavender:	Tumbleweed

Step Three: If you could be any magical creature, what would you be?

Unicorn:	The Round Table	The Sphinx:	The Great Pyramid
Elf:	Rivendell	Yeti:	The Himalayas
Dragon:	House Targaryen	Loch Ness Monster:	Clan Mackenzie
Paul Bunyan:	Minnesota	Witch:	Salem
Mermaid:	Atlantis	Cyclops:	Sicily
Vampire:	Transylvania	This book is stupid:	Beverly Hills

Now add it all together! _____ + _____

Of _____

I am Admiral Wombat of The Himalayas. From here on out, you shall address me as "Admiral Wombat of The Himalayas."

What's Your Distance Learning Personality?

The Really Awesome Quiz!

Have you ever looked around a waiting room to make sure no one was watching as you took a magazine quiz about your sexual prowess? Do you ever take the results of a personality quiz just a little too seriously? Have you ever kept changing your answers to an online quiz so you would not be placed in House Slytherin? If so, then this is the quiz for you! If not, who are you and what are you doing with this activity book?

1. It's 2 a.m. and you just remembered that you forgot to help your third grader study for their spelling test...

   a. Who needs spelling? Isn't that why we have autocorrect?

   b. Didn't everyone else have their kids memorize the dictionary for some light intellectual stimulation during summer vacation?

   c. Everybody up! Nobody sleeps until Junior has mastered the spelling list!

   d. I will torch the city if my child's teacher dares give him anything less than a 100% on a spelling quiz.

2. It's Back to School Night! On Zoom!

   a. What's Back to School Night?

   b. I prepared a slideshow for the teacher's presentation and a packet with helpful information and tips for the parents. I photocopied the packets at my own expense (it was just 87 pages per parent) and then hand delivered the packets to everyone's home so we can all be on the same page.

   c. What if the teacher hates me?! What if I ruin my kid's life???

   d. I polish my shotgun in plain view of my computer's camera.

3. The learning device issued by your child's school malfunctions:

   a. Far out. Beach day!

   b. I own several backup devices for this sort of eventuality and seamlessly swap in a new device so that my child does not miss a nanosecond of distance learning.

   c. Why me?! Why now?! Reboot! Reboot! It's not rebooting! My child is never getting into Harvard now! I have ruined her life! Oh why won't you reboot? For the love of all things holy, just reboot!!!

   d. I shoot the device with my shotgun and then have my people deliver a message to the Superintendent.

4. Your child is frustrated because it is hard to focus when the internet connection keeps kicking her out of Google Meets. You tell your child:

   a. Let's take the next month off of school. We can work on your bartending skills. Your martini is an embarrassment to the entire family.

   b. My child is never frustrated because I have a PhD in developmental psychology.

   c. I can't! I can't! I cannot process any more feelings! Too many feelings!

   d. I send my minions to the internet provider and they sort things out.

5. One of the kids in your child's class constantly interrupts the teacher, harasses the other students, and hacks into Google Meets and screens some troubling clips from *The Shining*. You think:

   a. I really like martinis.

   b. I will organize a petition, galvanize the PTA, and snuff out this nonsense. I will also send some brochures for military school to the brat's parents.

   c. Oh my god, oh my god, oh my god, I have to call my therapist. Where's my emergency chocolate?

   d. That's my kid! I could not be prouder.

6. The Superintendent sends an email announcing that in-person instruction will not begin for at least another three months. You:

a. Rejoice! Three more months of reenacting episodes of *The Floor Is Lava* with my kids!

b. Experience a flutter of disappointment, quickly snuff it out, and plan the next six months of supplementary curriculum so my child is ready to skip at least one grade (two would be better) by the time this is over.

c. Curl up in the fetal position beneath the kitchen table and refuse to come out for the next 36 hours.

d. Look up the Superintendent's home address.

7. Mid-semester, your child's school announces they are rolling out an exciting new learning platform:

a. Wait! Let me turn my body into a human bridge so you can crawl across me from the couch to the coffee table. Focus! The floor! Is! Lava!

b. I used my experience as a computer programmer to design the new learning platform. I will donate the royalties to charity.

c. What? Can they do that? I just figured out the old platform! My brain cannot handle a new one!

d. Someone is going to die.

8. Your child's report card indicates that she is struggling with math.

a. But just how important is subtraction?

b. That's not possible. The principal better fix this immediately. Nothing will tarnish my child's future!

c. I knew it. It's my fault. She got the "bad at math" genes from me.

d. I am going to teach that so-called teacher a lesson about what it means to struggle.

9. Your child's school is distributing art supplies:

a. Far out! Let's go get the art supplies! Has anyone seen my car keys? No? Nevermind. At least we tried.

b. I spearheaded the acquisition of art supplies and suggested a few projects based on my college internship at The Louvre.

c. We're late! Our pickup slot was from 11:00-11:20 and it's 11:21 and I can see the principal glaring at me.

d. We already got art supplies last month after a box fell off the back of a truck, if you know what I mean.

10. Distance learning is finally over:

a. We might as well miss the rest of this school year and start fresh in November. What? School starts in August?

b. Now I can reclaim my destiny as PTA President and whip this school back into shape.

c. I swear, these are happy tears.

d. Retribution will be swift.

And the Results...

Mostly As, Jeff Spicoli. Your equanimity is impressive but also a bit alarming. It might be time to accept your parents' offer to raise your kids.

Mostly Bs, Monica Geller. Calm down. You are making us all look bad. We do not need croquembouche at the bake sale.

Mostly Cs, Courtney Henning Novak. Calm down. Everyone is struggling. We all hate this.

Mostly Ds, Tony Soprano/Sauron. You are absolutely terrifying. Please don't kill me.

Distance Learning Wardrobe

Are you struggling to get dressed in the morning when your life has turned into the distance learning equivalent of *Groundhog Day*? Or does your "capsule wardrobe" need a little pizzaz? Then you need to play *The Distance Learning Wardrobe Game*!!!

To play, all you need is a ✏, 🎲 and your sense of humor! If you have lost your sense of humor during this ordeal (because you would have to be a saint not to) I suggest checking beneath your bed. That's where mine likes to hide.

For each category, roll the die (that's the singular form of dice, not a death threat) and then see what item corresponds with your roll. Write your answer on the line provided and then get dressed.

Tip: If you don't have the energy to raid the boardgames, just Google "roll dice" and you are all set.

Tops

⚀ T-shirt with coffee stain

⚁ T-shirt with mystery stain

⚂ Same thing I slept in

⚃ Pirate blouse

⚄ Button down for Zoom meeting

⚅ A wet towel

Oh fantastic, I'm wearing: _____

Bottoms

⚀ Jeans That Fit in March 2019

⚁ Kilt

⚂ Leggings so old, they are translucent

⚃ Unflattering overalls

⚄ Tutu

⚅ A wet towel

The inhumanity! I'm wearing: _____

Footwear

- ⚀ Mismatched socks
- ⚁ Fluffy bunny slippers
- ⚂ Those boots Julia Roberts wore in *Pretty Woman*
- ⚃ Are these mine?
- ⚄ Rainboots
- ⚅ The shoes that always give you blisters

Is Distance Learning over yet? _____

Outerwear

- ⚀ Superhero Cape
- ⚁ Witch Cape
- ⚂ Darth Vader Cape
- ⚃ Little Red Riding Hood Cape
- ⚄ Mr. Rogers' Cardigan
- ⚅ Wet Towel Cape

Is there a distance learning nudist colony?

_____

Accessories

- ⚀ Flamingo Sunglasses
- ⚁ Eyepatch
- ⚂ Wizard Staff
- ⚃ Fanny Pack
- ⚄ Button down for Zoom meeting
- ⚅ Marty McFly's Puffy Red Vest

This is actually making me feel better. No, wait. Sorry, that was just indigestion:

_____

I dare you to wear your new distance learning uniform to your next online school function. But if anyone gets weird about it, I will deny all responsibility.

Emotional Intelligence Matching Game

Draw a line from the emoji to the correct emotion. It does not have to be a straight line. Please do not play this game while operating heavy machinery or trying to understand Common Core math.

I thought I *was* smiling.

Trying to pretend I care. But I don't.

Going to Dentist! Get to ditch distance learning!

I'm not wearing pants today.

2019

Sad and Horrified

Eye hurts because got frustrated and stabbed myself with a pencil - that was stupid.

About. To. Blow. Up. Everything.

Seriously, who keeps playing *Jumanji*?

Panda

What day is it? Who am I?
What's the point of all this? Can I get a refund?

Check, highlight or X the squares as you "earn" them. Be the first to BINGO and watch your soul disintegrate into a heap of ash.

BINGO

Tell child's teacher how much you hate distance learning	Criticize the dingbats that organized D.L. for child's school	Can I get a refund on property taxes?	Therapy. Is. Not. Helping.	Wonder how much school child can miss before government appears on your doorstep
Completely lose track of the seasons	Feel heart crack open when school reopening delayed again	Total, absolute, all-consuming exasperation	Move to Idaho	Child's device crashes 5x in one hour
Hide from children in bathroom	Check status of public schools in Nebraska	Child in Distance Learning	Threaten child with no t.v. & immediately regret your stupidity	Overwhelmed by all the new technology, passwords, etc.
Fall on knees & beg for mercy	Bribe child to pay attention to teacher	Realize child has been wearing same clothes for 72 hours	Enlist grandparent's help. Break grandparent's spirit.	Is it too late to join the Amish?
Seriously consider home schooling	Is math necessary for a life of organized crime?	Folding laundry must be educational!	Take vow of silence and join monastery	Local natural disaster. WTF?

Would You Rather...???

Have your child unmute their mic when you are using your "scary voice"

OR

Do your grocery shopping buck naked

Extend distance learning for an extra five years

OR

Amputate the digit of your choice

Listen to a recording of a kindergarten class doing live distance learning on endless repeat for 72 hours

OR

Never eat dessert again. That includes chocolate. And ice cream.

Oversee a pod of a dozen first graders in your home

OR

Move to Alaska. Forever.

Have your child tell their class you are in the bathroom because you have diarrhea

OR

Give up your smartphone for a week

Help your child with math

OR

Only drink warm milk for the rest of your life

Be in charge of troubleshooting tech problems for your entire school district

OR

Go over Niagara Falls in a bucket

Teach online health class for high school students. Translation: Sex Ed.

OR

Teach online math class to second graders. Translation: Common Core Math.

Accidentally let your child's class see you without pants

OR

Only eat tapioca pudding for the rest of your life

Be involved with your child's distance learning experience

OR

Make a snarky activity book for parents just barely holding on to their last shred of sanity

Be elected by your fellow parents to tell the Parent of the Annoying Kid that her child is really, really freaking annoying

OR

Pay the Annoying Kid an exorbitant bribe to just mute his mic for the love of all things holy and sacred

Organize an online Christmas party for your child's second grade class

OR

Buy your child expensive Christmas gifts to compensate for shattered hopes and dreams

Spearhead a distance learning drama club for the school

OR

Dance with the devil in the pale moonlight

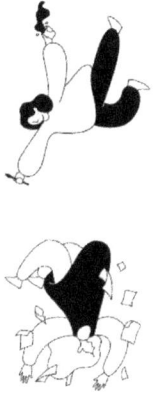

Have your child's computer/tablet crash at least once per hour

OR

Step on a rusty nail

Have the sound on your child's computer/tablet malfunction whenever the teacher is giving important directions

OR

Homeschool your child until this abomination is over

Be in charge of fundraising during distance learning

OR

Set fire to your hair

Distance Learning Yoga

Stressed? Anxious? Welcome to distance learning! The next time you feel your adrenaline racing, take a deep breath and try a few yoga poses. Maybe you can trick your central nervous system into thinking everything is okay.

"Just Standing Here, Staring Out Into Space, Because My Brain Is Completely Fried" Pose

Downward Goes My Soul Dog

Namaste Far Away From Distance Learning

Backward They Make My Soul Bend

"Would Rather Walk The Plank" Pose

"This Sh*t Would Make A Warrior Beg For Mercy" Pose

"I'm Stuck But Don't
Help Me Because I
Want To Stay Here
And Die" Pose

"No Bra, Prisoner of
My Own Home"
Pose

Chair Rhymes
with Despair

"I Broke The Internet
So I'd Have Time For
Yoga" Pose

Tree Of Eternal
Anguish

"My Brain Is
Even More
Twisted" Pose

"I Am Going To Stay
Here And Weep Quietly
Until This Travesty Is
Over" Pose

"Having Ice Cream
After This" Pose.

Not A Pose.
Actually A Corpse.

Rank The Evils!

Get excited, parents! It's time to play *Rank The Distance Learning Evils*! Rank the evils below from 1 to 16, 1 being "The Most Truly Evil Part Of Distance Learning" and 16 being "The Least Evil Part Of Distance Learning."

I know, I know. *Why are there sixteen evils to rank? Why not twenty? Or ten? Those are such lovely round numbers. Sixteen is awkward.* ARE YOU SERIOUSLY COMPLAINING THAT SIXTEEN IS AN AWKWARD NUMBER? You know what is awkward? DISTANCE LEARNING. Please do not suggest that ranking sixteen evils as opposed to ten or twenty is the thing that is going to push you over the edge. (Though now that you mention it, this actually might be the thing that does me in...)

☐ My kids are always home.

☐ Math.

☐ They are always hungry. How can one person need so much food?

☐ Being interrupted every other minute for a crisis that is not actually a crisis but if I do not attend to the crisis immediately, my child's head might actually explode.

☐ Constant nagging sense that everyone else is handling distance learning a thousand times better than me. I must be a bad parent because I wish my kids could go back to school already.

☐ Specter of impending doom marring the horizon.

☐ Getting my kids ready for school WHEN THEY DON'T ACTUALLY GO TO SCHOOL.

☐ I take the Fifth.

☐ The cheerful emails from the principal that suggest everything is going swimmingly well.

☐ Fear that my kids are going to be permanently messed up by this experience but man, therapy is really expensive. If I send my kids to therapy, will I be able to afford *my* therapist? What if I just get them a really nice stress ball?

☐ Concern that other parents are judging me for: (a) not doing enough to support the distance learning experience; (b) being way too involved and making everyone else look bad; or (c) making some questionable fashion choices in the 90s but seriously guys, fanny packs are really useful.

☐ THEY HAVE DESTROYED MY HOME. Look, I know Marie Kondo was never going to give me a prize for "Tidiest Home" but you would not believe what has happened since school was cancelled. I think we might have lost a couch? I don't want to know the source of the suspicious stains on the wall. And the toys are multiplying to prepare for the Robot Revolution.

☐ Make believe. Since my kids are not seeing their friends, they are desperate for a make believe companion AND ALL I WANT TO DO IS STAGE THE VIOLENT EXECUTION OF ALL THE BARBIES.

☐ Red rum! Red rum!

☐ Hope. I keep hoping things will get better and then the Superintendent tramples all over my hopes and dreams until they resemble roadkill.

☐ When I look in the mirror, and I see the feral look in my eyes, and I realize, *My kids can see that I have completely lost my mind. Their future therapist is going to think I'm a monster.*

Let's Plan A Fantasy Vacation!

You know what you need? A vacation from the Distance Learning S-Show. You know what you are not going to get? A vacation from the Distance Learning S-Show. But we can still plan a fantasy vacation! If you are feeling lazy, just check the box for the option that sounds best. If you are feeling more ambitious: (1) it might be time to reevaluate your caffeine intake, but (2) there are lines for you to jot down your schemes and dreams.

Step One: When Will You Go?

☐ Immediately, if not sooner!

☐ The day before distance learning started. I will find a time machine. This is not a problem.

☐ Never. I'm too broken to even dream.

☐ Tomorrow.

☐ Next month. I need something to live for.

☐ Am I really allowed to think about something so magical as a vacation?

Or choose your own time frame, but seriously, less caffeine tomorrow, m'kay?

Step Two: Who Will Go With You?

☐ No one. I desperately crave solitude.

☐ My family! Because yes! We need to spend even more time together!

☐ Dame Maggie Smith.

☐ Friends. My family is sick of me. The feeling is mutual.

☐ Kermit the Frog.

☐ Literally anyone so long as it means I get to leave this emotional wasteland.

Or choose your own sidekick/accomplice, but seriously, you are not getting extra credit for this:

Step Three: Where Will You Go?

☐ Someplace tropical.

☐ The Alaskan wilderness where I can prepare for the Zombie Apocalypse that must be coming.

☐ Somewhere over the rainbow.

☐ A galaxy far, far away.

☐ Literally anywhere so long as distance learning is banned.

☐ South Dakota.

Or choose your own destination, and you know what? This is a fantasy vacation, so you can pretend there is no pandemic and everywhere and anywhere is fair play.

Step Four: Choose Your Accommodations

☐ A hammock slung between palm trees on the beach.

☐ Luxury underground bunker with ample supply of toilet paper, canned goods, garlic and a well-sharpened stake.

☐ In a temporary art installation outside the Guggenheim that explores the intersection between the void of distance learning and the collective sense of futility - I don't know what that means, but the artist said there's a hot tub.

☐ The Four Seasons, bitches.

☐ My personal Airstream. That will look good on Instagram and I want everyone I know to be jealous.

☐ The Witness Protection Program says that intelligence is classified.

Or choose your own accommodations if you really think you can do better than the Four Seasons.

Is there distance learning in Vegas??? Asking for a friend...

Step Five: What Will You Pack?

☐ Whatever is clean and still fits after all the stress eating.

☐ My kids can pack for me. I don't care what I wear, so long as I get to go.

☐ Night vision goggles, crossbow, and a bullet proof vest. It's probably best if you don't ask questions.

☐ Feather boa, novelty sunglasses, and a safari vest.

☐ Everything black because I am in mourning for the life I once had.

☐ Toga!

Need anything else? A huge stack of trashy romance novels? A tandem bicycle? Boogie board? A hammock and flame thrower? No one is judging you if you bring all your supplies for making balloon animals. (Okay, that's a lie. We are judging you. But you do you.)

_____

_____

Step Six: How Will Your Travel?

☐ Limousine driven by Kevin Bacon.

☐ That train from *The Hunger Games* but instead of Woody Harrelson, I get to hang with Octavia Spencer because she just seems like a really good person to meet on a train.

☐ Covered wagon. Who wants to play *Oregon Trail*?!

☐ Private jet flown by Kevin Bacon.

☐ That submarine at Disneyland except fuck Nemo, we are hunting for Red October.

☐ *His name is Clyde.*

You really need to lay off the expresso, Capt. Overachiever.

_____

_____

I have some extra space so instead of an awkwardly large margin, I thought I'd share some fun facts about sloths. Sloths are related to armadillos and anteaters. They spend most of their lives upside down. They even mate and give birth upside down! I learned that while helping Pippa research her animal report for second grade. I did not tell her about the mating and giving birth bit. We focused on the giant sloth, instead, which was the size of an elephant and went extinct about 12,000 years ago.

Step Seven: What Will You Do On Vacation?

☐ Lounge in the pool with a drink served inside a pineapple.

☐ Stare vacantly into space and drool.

☐ Go ziplining, snorkeling, hiking, and surfing to burn away the memories of distance learning.

☐ All the spa treatments.

☐ What happens in Vegas, stays in Vegas.

☐ Visit an anger room where I can break all the things. I saw it on an episode of *Billions* so it must be real.

Go ahead. Go crazy. It's your fantasy vacation. It's never going to happen but it's okay to daydream for a few minutes, even if your child is screaming about some issue with the internet.

_____

_____

_____

Step Eight: How Long Will This Vacation Last?

☐ I just need a long weekend and I'll be ready to tackle distance learning again.

☐ Two weeks, maybe three weeks, oh well, might as well round up to a month.

☐ Until distance learning is over.

☐ Strongly considering faking my death and never returning. What are the moral implications?

☐ Until I extinguish the last vampire.

☐ I'm sorry, what were we doing? Is there an activity? Do I have to submit this to my child's teacher?

Last chance for extra credit! I'd make a snarky remark, but my brain is tired.

_____

Thank you for joining me for this activity. It's time to return to distance learning now. Please, release your death grip on my leg. Oh no, stop crying. I didn't mean that. Go ahead. Stay attached to my leg like some maniacal koala. We can watch *Tiger King* again if that makes you feel better.

The Distance Learning Survey Your Child's School Does Not Have The Nerve To Send

Our school district has sent several surveys since this debacle started. In theory, the surveys were meant to elicit helpful information to improve the distance learning experience. In actuality, they only sought just enough information to give the appearance that the Authorities care about the students while avoiding the questions that really need to be asked. Here at last, we have the survey that the schools would send if they actually cared about our sanity.

Read the questions and fill in the bubble that best corresponds with your true feelings. Do not hold back. No one with the power to improve distance learning will ever see your answers because they are too busy writing their next evasive email update.

Use the scale below for your responses. I will post the scale with every question because it is funny and took me a long time to make.

1. Distance learning is fun!

Agree! Yay! Denial!	Will reluctantly agree as soon as my bribe arives.	Seriously?	No! Non! Nein!	Beware my wrath. Vengeance will be swift.
①	②	③	④	⑤

2. The quality of education that my child is receiving with distance learning is nearly as good as the education she would have received in person.

Agree! Yay! Denial!	Will reluctantly agree as soon as my bribe arives.	Seriously?	No! Non! Nein!	Beware my wrath. Vengeance will be swift.
①	②	③	④	⑤

3. Distance learning is going so well, the kids probably never need to go back to school!

Agree! Yay! Denial!	Will reluctantly agree as soon as my bribe arives.	Seriously?	No! Non! Nein!	Beware my wrath. Vengeance will be swift.
①	②	③	④	⑤

4. Your child finds online interactions with classmates to be rewarding, meaningful and stimulating.

Agree! Yay! Denial!	Will reluctantly agree as soon as my bribe arives.	Seriously?	No! Non! Nein!	Beware my wrath. Vengeance will be swift.
①	②	③	④	⑤

5. Distance-learning has deepened the bond with your child and you are incredibly grateful to have been blessed with this experience.

Agree! Yay! Denial!	Will reluctantly agree as soon as my bribe arives.	Seriously?	No! Non! Nein!	Beware my wrath. Vengeance will be swift.
①	②	③	④	⑤

6. You are impressed with how seamless the transition from regular school to distance learning was.

Agree! Yay! Denial!	Will reluctantly agree as soon as my bribe arives.	Seriously?	No! Non! Nein!	Beware my wrath. Vengeance will be swift.
①	②	③	④	⑤

7. You are so relieved you do not have to deal with school lunches anymore. We actually did you a big favor by switching to distance learning. Your welcome.

Agree! Yay! Denial!	Will reluctantly agree as soon as my bribe arives.	Seriously?	No! Non! Nein!	Beware my wrath. Vengeance will be swift.
1	2	3	4	5

8. The platforms we are using to run distance learning have never made you want to rip off your eyebrows.

Agree! Yay! Denial!	Will reluctantly agree as soon as my bribe arives.	Seriously?	No! Non! Nein!	Beware my wrath. Vengeance will be swift.
1	2	3	4	5

9. This experience has never made you question your sanity or doubt your parenting skills. You were born for distance learning.

Agree! Yay! Denial!	Will reluctantly agree as soon as my bribe arives.	Seriously?	No! Non! Nein!	Beware my wrath. Vengeance will be swift.
1	2	3	4	5

10. Distance learning has not had a negative effect on your expected life span. In fact, it has probably improved your overall health and wellness.

Agree! Yay! Denial!	Will reluctantly agree as soon as my bribe arives.	Seriously?	No! Non! Nein!	Beware my wrath. Vengeance will be swift.
1	2	3	4	5

11. Distance learning does not interfere with your ability to do your work, run the household, exercise, and have meaningful conversations with other adults.

Agree! Yay! Denial!	Will reluctantly agree as soon as my bribe arives.	Seriously?	No! Non! Nein!	Beware my wrath. Vengeance will be swift.
①	②	③	④	⑤

12. You are excited to donate to fundraising requests.

Agree! Yay! Denial!	Will reluctantly agree as soon as my bribe arives.	Seriously?	No! Non! Nein!	Beware my wrath. Vengeance will be swift.
①	②	③	④	⑤

13. You are not counting the days until this is over. Speaking of which, you embrace uncertainty and do not need to know when your child will return to school.

Agree! Yay! Denial!	Will reluctantly agree as soon as my bribe arives.	Seriously?	No! Non! Nein!	Beware my wrath. Vengeance will be swift.
①	②	③	④	⑤

14. We have done a superb job of soliciting your feedback and you can tell we are genuinely concerned about your sanity and the quality of your child's education.

Agree! Yay! Denial!	Will reluctantly agree as soon as my bribe arives.	Seriously?	No! Non! Nein!	Beware my wrath. Vengeance will be swift.
①	②	③	④	⑤

A List Of Things Purchased In The Desperate Hope They Might Make This Experience Slightly Tolerable

It is time to unburden your soul and confess your retail therapy sins. Place a ✪ or ♡ or 🐧 next to any items that were severely disappointing.

Since we are friends now, here's my list:

- UNGODLY NUMBER OF SECOND GRADE WORKBOOKS
- SOMEWHAT LESS UNGODLY NUMBER OF PRESCHOOL WORKBOOKS (BUT STILL ABSURD)
- TAP DANCE SHOES (FOR ME, DUH)
- RESISTANCE BANDS
- PURPLE WALKING SHOES ✪
- 5 TIER PLASTIC DESK ORGANIZER ✪
- LAVENDER ESSENTIAL OIL
- UNICORN WIG
- ZOLOFT
- SO MANY PLANTS
- PINK TUTU SKIRT ✪
- YARN

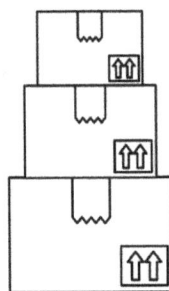

Now it's your turn!

Pro Tip: I scrolled through my Purchase History for Amazon for the last six months to compile my list.

_____

_____

_____

_____

_____

_____

_____

Think your list is stranger than mine? Take a pic and send it to courtneyhenningnovak@gmail.com or IG@courtney.novak.
We'll let my husband Nathan be the judge.
This will probably irritate him immensely. Excellent.

Word Scramble Affirmations

Unscramble the phrases below to discover some inspiring affirmations that you can say while gazing into your reflection in the mirror. The affirmations will probably not make you feel better, but at least this activity will help you fill the next ten to fifteen minutes of your life, and when you are done, you will be ten to fifteen minutes closer to the end of distance learning, whenever that might be.

HSIT SI A LATTO FCKU, TUB TA LAEST I MA OTN A PIVAMRE.

_____

_____

SCENATDI RNINGAEL SI TON HET PCAPYLESA. TI UJTS ESEMS HATH YAW.

_____

_____

I OOSHCE OT EEELRSA OIHSTYLIT, VATAGGRAION NAD NTOI HET ROWDL DAYOT.

_____

_____

"Remember to breathe. One deep breath should be all you need to survive distance learning." No One, Never.

I DIRATEA UIQTE REPIODESAONT OT LAL I EMET.

_____

_____

I VIGE YSMLEF PCASE OT SEOL LAL YM TSIHS.

_____

_____

I IGVE FELSMLY MREIONSSIP OT TAE LAL HET OWEALLHEN ANCYD.

_____

_____

Answer Key: Did you think I would leave you without a way to cheat? I know your brain is fried enough by distance learning. I do not want to add to your distress! (Hint: flip book over to read the upside down answers. Seriously, I know how fried your brain is.)

I give myself permission to eat all the Halloween candy.
I give myself space to lose all my shits.
I choose to release hostility, aggravation and angst into the world today.
I radiate quiet desperation to all I meet.
Distance learning is not the apocalypse. It just seems that way.
This is a total fuck, but at least I am not a vampire.

Welcome to intermission! Elphaba has just defied gravity! No wizard is going to bring her down! Quick, ladies, run to the bathroom before the line is longer than the wait for Space Mountain (assuming Gavin Newsom ever lets Disneyland reopen) (and also, I know Space Mountain has been renamed, something with a *Star Wars* name, and I love the addition of *Star Wars* music to the ride, but I am always going to call it Space Mountain).

Do you guys remember when the original *Star Wars* trilogy was rereleased into theaters in the 90s? I was in high school. There was an epic line to get into the Fox theater in Westwood. Once we were allowed inside, everyone rushed to the bathrooms, and for the first time in the history of movie theaters, the line for the men's room was a mile long and there was no line for the women's restroom. My friends and I pointed and cackled as we walked by the men.

I digress.

During this intermission, you might want to get up, stretch your legs, and check the fridge for interesting distractions. Or maybe you want to listen to *Defying Gravity* and pretend you can sing as well as Idina Menzel. I would listen to that lady sing the phone book out loud. Heck, I'd listen to her sing *Baby Shark* and then that song about what the fox says. Ok, look sharp. Intermission is over! I think you are going to love the next activity.

It's Mascot Time!

Do you know what you need? I mean, aside from an all expenses paid trip to Tahiti for the next five years, a lifetime supply of sticky notes, and A SCHOOL THAT IS ACTUALLY OPEN. You need a mascot! Mascots are all the rage with baseball teams, colleges and fast food chains. Do you think Kool-Aid would be half as delicious as it is without the Kool-Aid Man? Of course not!

It is time to get yourself a Distance Learning Mascot. Choose from any or all of the options on this and the following pages. Color your new mascot or leave it black and white for a film noir vibe. Then cut it out carefully or have your offspring cut it out for you and call it Distance Learning Art.

Now, here is where you can get fancy. If you are an uber-nerd like me, laminate your mascot! (I cannot believe it took me this long to mention lamination.) Or, you can glue your mascot to cardstock or even cardboard to give it some extra substance. Tape a popsicle stick or pretty straw to the back and stick your mascot in a houseplant, an empty coffee can, or with your toothbrushes. But don't feel obligated to be fancy on my account! You can also just tape your mascot to the wall - maybe in the room where you like to have nervous breakdowns? Or tuck it into your wallet as a reminder that you are not alone in this distance learning insanity. YOU HAVE A MASCOT!

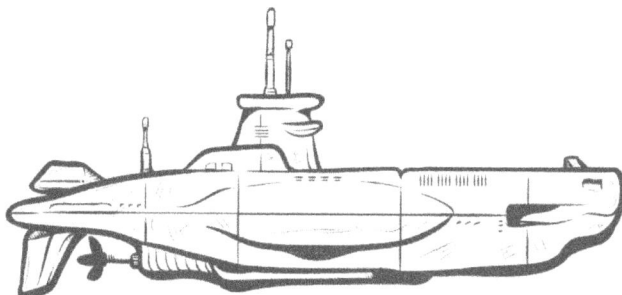

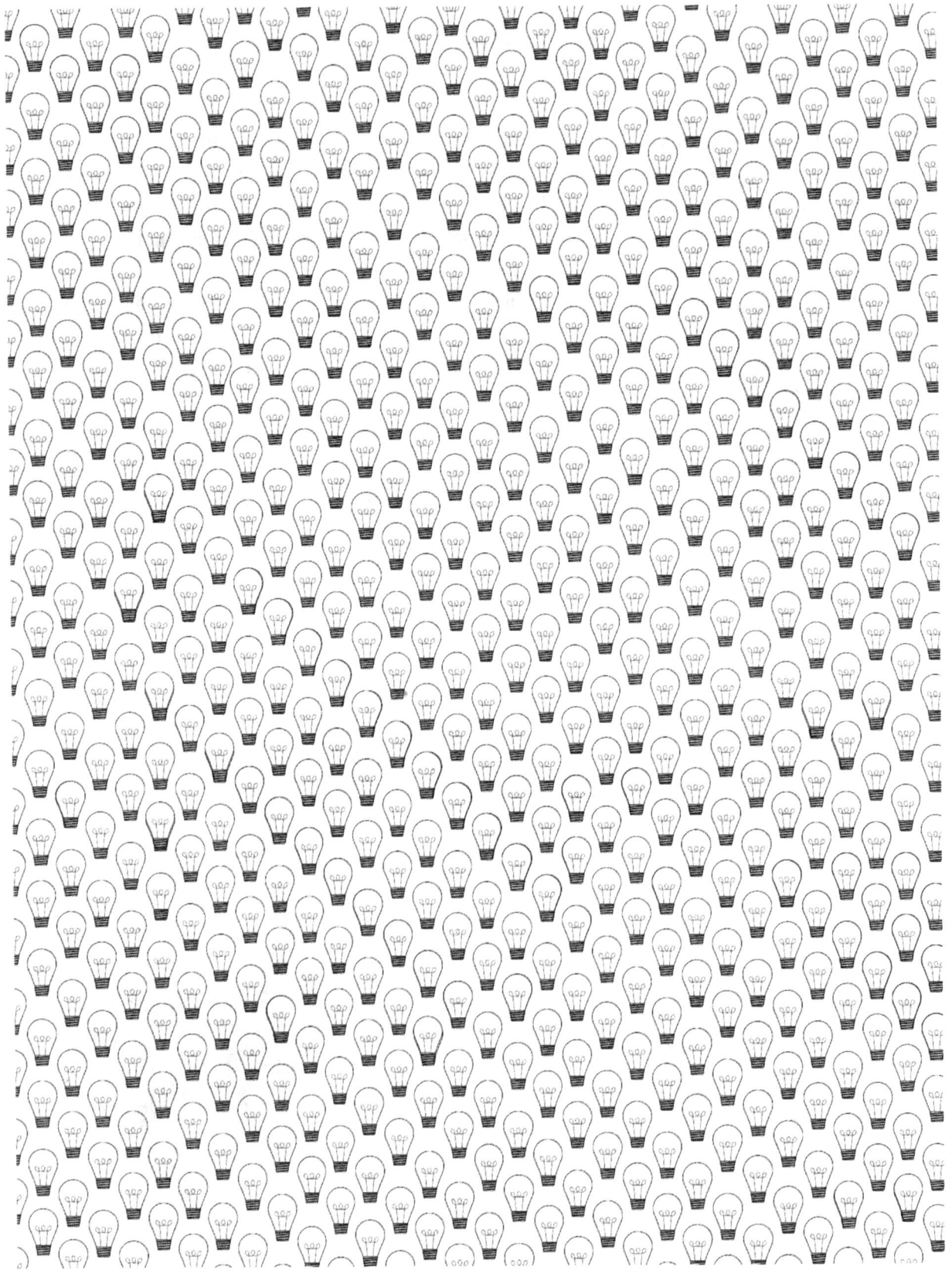

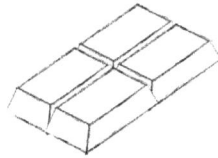
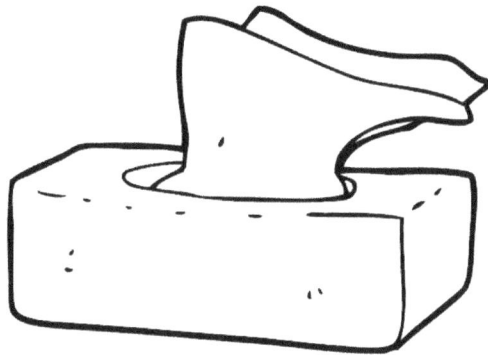

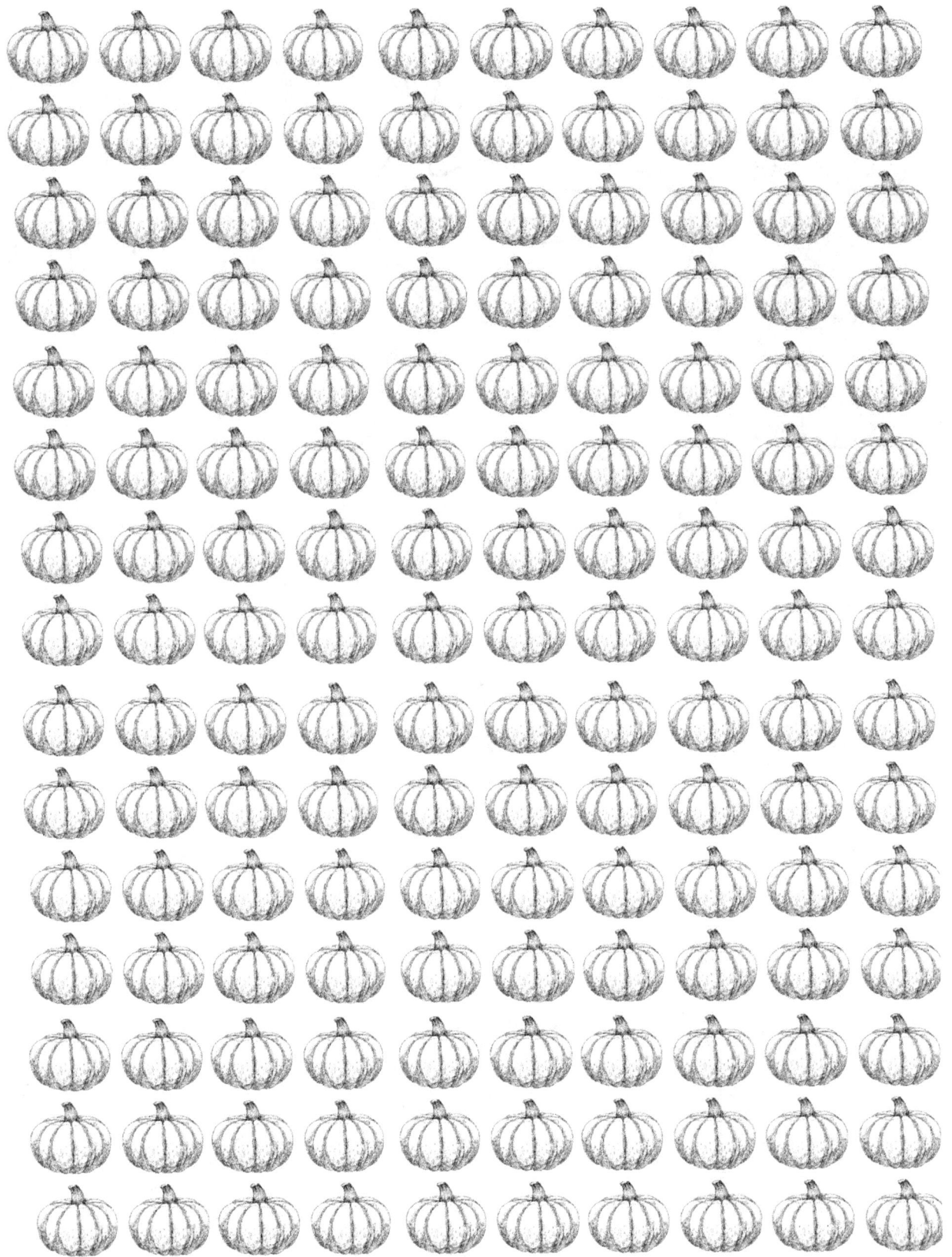

It Could Be Worse!

Circle all the pictures that depict a scenario that would be worse than distance learning. Cross out the ones that would be a vast improvement over the distance learning calamity. Feel free to color these pictures first if that would make you feel better. Or just burn the book. Whatever keeps you sane...

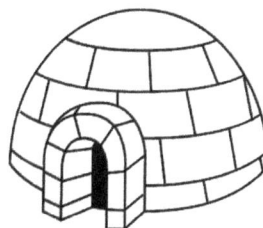

Conversation Starters

Distance learning has diminished our brain power. Or maybe our brains have just decided to go on hiatus until this debacle is over. (Can you blame them?) (Oh how I wish I could take a sabbatical...) Either way, when we try to say something intelligible, words might come out of our mouths, but said words are not always strung together into coherent thoughts.

Also, when it comes to conversation, many of us are grossly out of practice. Instead of going to work and talking to actual adults or chatting with our fellow parents in the preschool parking lot, we are prisoners of distance learning.

As opportunities for conversation arise, you might be elated at the chance to interact with a human that does not live in your home, but you also might get overwhelmed and not know what to say. Do not panic! You are not alone. Just memorize these handy dandy conversation starters, and before you know it, you'll be having conversations that make your soul sparkle.

Conversation With A Parent You Have Not Seen In Ages:
- On a scale of 1 to 10, how much do you despise distance learning?
- Have you discovered any counter-curses to negate the emotional toll of distance learning?
- What dark forces do you think are behind this debacle?
- Do you know what day of the week it is? Okay, what about the month?
- Is it okay if I cry now? Because I'm going to cry.
- Do you have any idea what this thing on my toe might be?
- You do not look like you have aged too much. Can you recommend a moisturizer?

Is it weird that I am jealous about the lack of social distancing and face masks? Because I am

Conversation With The Parent Of The Annoying Kid:
- Do you hate your child as much as I do?
- Have you considered military school?
- Are you actively encouraging your child to disrupt the lesson as much as possible?
- You know I'm judging you, right?
- Why is your kid so awful?

Conversation With Another Parent When You Need To Talk About Something More Pleasant Than Distance Learning:

- Have you ever gone swimming with sharks?
- When the Zombie Apocalypse begins, whose side are you going to take?
- Have you ever had a colonoscopy?
- I like bagels. What about you?
- Do you think our Robot Overlords will be kind?

Conversation With Your Child's Teacher:

- Just how necessary to life success is math?
- Will my child still be able to go to college if I mostly neglect distance learning and make a snarky activity book about distance learning instead?
- How do you do this year after year after year without resorting to sex, drugs and rock and roll?

Conversation With Your Neighbor:

- Hypothetically speaking, do you ever hear anyone screaming like a banshee?
- Would you describe my outfit as chic or vagabond?
- Do you suspect that any of our fellow neighbors might be in league with the devil?
- Can I have all your ketchup?

Conversation With Parents When You Are Planning A Rebellion Because Seriously, It Is Time To End This Fiasco Already:

- Who owns a flamethrower?
- Have you sharpened your pitchforks recently?
- What if we just leave all our kids at school on Monday morning and see what happens?
- Does anyone have a spare brain?

Some final tips:

- It is okay to cry. It is not okay to use the other party's shirt as a tissue.
- Absolutely no barking.
- Avoid sounding like Hannibal Lecter, Snow White or Donald Trump.

True or False?

The Distance Learning Edition

For every statement, answer True, False, WTF or FTS (Fuck this shit). This is an actual test. You will be graded. The fate of humanity depends on your grade. No, I cannot tell you what that means. Just take the test.

1. I am enjoying the opportunities for personal growth created by the absurdity that is distance learning. _____

2. My school district has really been acing this whole distance learning thing. _____

3. Distance learning has mangled my soul and turned it into an unreconizable lump of goo. _____

π. Pumpkin pie is overrated. _____

4. Tomorrow will be better. _____

5. Yesterday was not so bad. _____

6. I often have to resist the urge to do extreme violence to my child's learning device. _____

7. If this is a cosmic joke, I'm still waiting for the punchline. _____

8. My mental health has not suffered during this exciting season of life. _____

9. I will do cartwheels and backflips (imaginary or real) when my child goes back to school. _____

(10) I have become intimately familiar with the contours of despair, agony and frustration. _____

(11) My therapist taught me some breathing techniques that have helped me feel centered and grounded throughout this adventure. _____

(12) Antartica is sounding better and better every day. _____

(13) My soul requires daily infusions of ice cream in order to suppress homicidal tendencies. _____

(14) This experience has brought to my attention some truly terrifying demons that were lurking in my subconscious. _____

(15) Multitasking is awesome! _____

(16) A newborn who wakes up to feed every two hours is suddenly looking like a cake walk. _____

(17) This keeps getting easier as the months fly by. _____

(18) I'm not wearing underpants. _____

(19) *The Shining* is not fiction. It is a documentary about what happens to parents when they are locked away from humanity and forced to act excited about distance learning. _____

(20) On the bright side, at least I will never again run out of things to say to my therapist. _____

Extra Credit: Make photocopies of your finished test and mail it to your Superintendent, principal, local newspaper, and the parent of the really annoying kid in your child's class. They will think you are crazy, but you will feel like you have accomplished something. Not a big something. Not a helpful something. But *something*, and we all deserve to feel like we have some agency over our lives, even if it's just an illusion that lasts for the amount of time it takes you to address the envelope and find a stamp.

Will Today Be A Good Day?

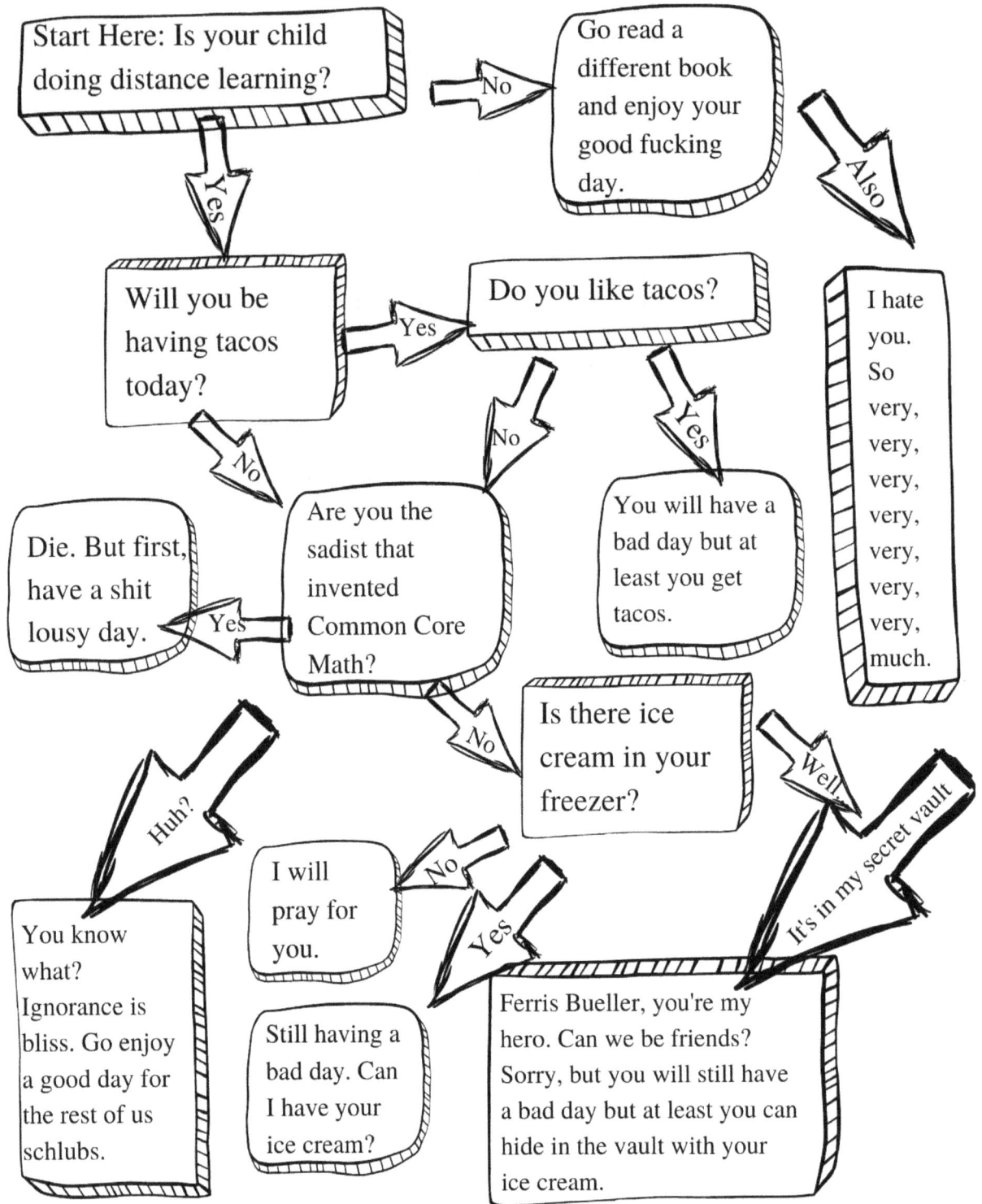

Start Here: Is your child doing distance learning?

No → Go read a different book and enjoy your good fucking day.

Also → I hate you. So very, very, very, very, very, very, very, much.

Yes ↓

Will you be having tacos today?

Yes → Do you like tacos?

No → Are you the sadist that invented Common Core Math?

Do you like tacos?

No → Are you the sadist that invented Common Core Math?

Yes → You will have a bad day but at least you get tacos.

Will you be having tacos today?

No → Die. But first, have a shit lousy day.

Are you the sadist that invented Common Core Math?

Yes → Die. But first, have a shit lousy day.

No → Is there ice cream in your freezer?

Are you the sadist that invented Common Core Math?

Huh? → You know what? Ignorance is bliss. Go enjoy a good day for the rest of us schlubs.

Is there ice cream in your freezer?

No → I will pray for you.

Yes → Ferris Bueller, you're my hero. Can we be friends? Sorry, but you will still have a bad day but at least you can hide in the vault with your ice cream.

Well → (Is there ice cream in your freezer?)

It's in my secret vault → Ferris Bueller, you're my hero. Can we be friends? Sorry, but you will still have a bad day but at least you can hide in the vault with your ice cream.

I will pray for you. → Still having a bad day. Can I have your ice cream?

Help!

Prunella is headed to the grocery store but her kids have wrecked the house and she can't find her phone. It looks like this ▯ and she just wants to scroll mindlessly on social media while waiting in the checkout line. Can you help her find it? For bonus points, see if you can also find a tooth, one roller skate, two ants, three croissants and the source of that god awful smell.

The Marriage Vows We Actually Needed

Hindsight is 20/20, but sweet Beelzebub, my wedding vows were not designed for the horror that is distance learning. For better or worse? Sickness and health? Richer and poorer? Child's play! Going forward, all wedding vows should be updated and expanded to include distance learning. If you and your honey are already wed, and 2020 has not made you seriously entertain the idea of getting divorced, perhaps you would like to update your wedding vows to get you through these dark times. You can also exchange these vows with your best friend, your child's teacher, the principal or some random stranger you accost. Or, if you are on suboptimal terms with your child's other parent, feel free to write some bitter ass vows and then toast yourself with a glass of champagne. For inspiration, I have included my vows below.

I, Courtney, take you, Nathan, to be my wedded Distance Learning Partner in Crime, to have and to hold, from this day forward, for better, for worse, and really insanely worst case scenario, in sickness and health and pandemic, even when we are forced to stay at home for weeks and weeks on end with no end in sight as we drag our sorry asses across the distance learning finish line, even when the internet collapses and our child throws a tantrum because she just want to go back to school already. I will not make you handle all the math, though probably most of it, because you are better at math than me, and now that I really think about it, I'm going to need you to handle all of the math for both our sakes. I promise to cherish you even when you are in a lousy mood, and when I am in a vile mood, I will try not to take it out on you, though we both know I will fail at that miserably. If you make me popcorn, I promise to do most of my crying in the shower. I will be your alibi if you are ever forced to take drastic measures to cope with distance learning, and I will look the other way if you get so angry, you need to beat a cactus with a shovel. Til death or distance learning, do us part, whichever comes first, which will probably be death, because Blessed Virgin, this is never going to end.

Now it's your turn! Dim the lights, pour the champagne or Le Croix, and turn on your favorite wedding tunes. Bonus points if you use a ridiculous pen that has glittery feathers.

Distance Learning Self-Portrait

Embellish and color the portrait below to create your distance learning self-portrait. Remember to include stress zits, new wrinkles, bags under the eyes, grey hairs, and scratch marks from your frustrated child. The next page has a few suggestions if your brain is just too broken for this much creativity...

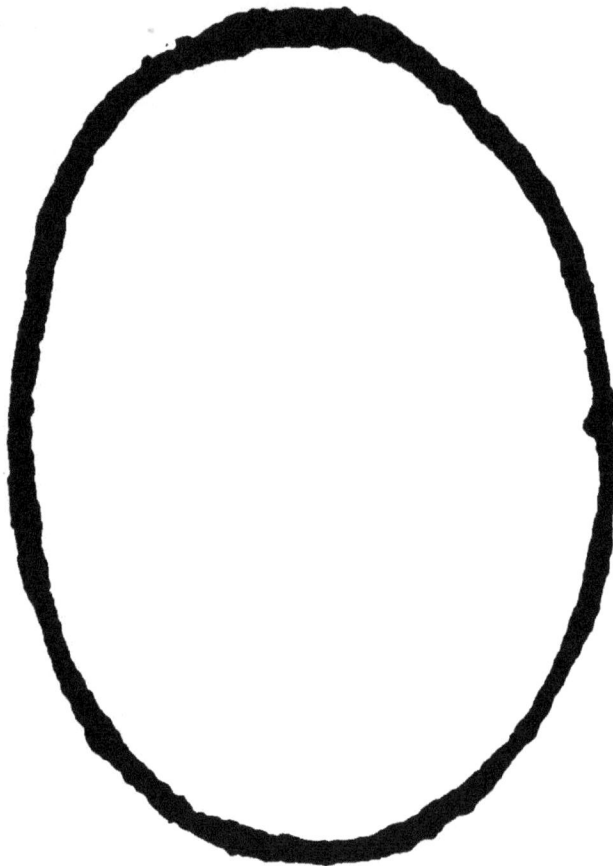

Self-Portrait Cheat Sheet

Single Tear

Actually Dead

Acne

Olaf

Creepy Clown Nose

Denial

Gandalf Beard

Let's bring back monocles!

Yearbook Superlatives

Let's pretend we are making a Distance Learning Yearbook. The superlatives are the best part of any respectable yearbook. Now you get to nominate the people in your life who should receive these very special distinctions and honors. You can nominate ANYONE: fellow parents, teachers, students, the principal, the superintendent, ANYONE THIS IS YOUR ACTIVITY BOOK BE BOLD BE WILD BE CRAZY FORGET GRAMMAR AND GO COMMANDO!

Most likely to fail spectacularly at distance learning:

_____

Most likely to spontaneously combust:

_____

Most likely to unmute their mic and harass the teacher despite repeated requests to mute their goddamn mic:

_____

Most likely to never read any emails from the teacher, principal and other parents and then get royally pissed when child does not have supplies for the craft project:

_____

Carpe diem!   what a great year!   life is good   GOOD THINGS AHEAD   Believe in yourself

Most likely to move to New Zealand because they just can't do this anymore:

_____

Most likely to condemn this book as filth and heresy:

_____

Most likely to scream at the principal:

_____

Most likely to use PTA Zoom meeting as a platform for selling essential oils and leggings:

_____

Most likely to strike a deal with the devil to end the abomination that is distance learning:

_____

Most likely to be recognized as a saint for making distance learning somewhat vaguely tolerable:

_____

DO what you LOVE   Keep going   What a great Year!   Say Cheese   Better Days AHEAD   BE positive

Most annoying parent/child couple:

_____

Most likely to have own reality show one day:

_____

Most in denial about the horrors of this hellscape:

_____

Most likely to get divorced first:

_____

Most likely to betray us all to the vampires:

_____

Most likely to go viral with a rant about distance learning:

_____

Best supportive listener during a rant about the unreasonable expectations being imposed by the bureaucrats who designed our distance learning program:

_____

Most likely to invent a new way of teaching math that is even worse than Common Core math:

_____

Most likely to overthrow the School Board, negotiate with the Teachers' Union and get the kids back to school:

_____

Most likely to break her child's laptop/tablet on purpose by setting fire to it in front of City Hall:

_____

Best at saying mean things to the teacher in a way that seems polite and respectful:

_____

Favorite person to judge because come on, we need some sort of way to make ourselves feel better:

_____

Most likely to sob uncontrollably in public when this horror show is over and we can forget about the pandemic and not wear masks and let our children enjoy their childhood:

_____

Zoom Scavenger Hunt

Have you ever found your mind wandering during a school-related Zoom event? Do you begin to question the meaning of life during the first five minutes of an online meeting? Then it's time to go on a Zoom scavenger hunt! Try to check off as many boxes below during your next Zoom meeting. If an authority figure suspects you are having too much fun, tell them that Courtney is a bad influence. (Don't worry, it won't be the first time that has happened.)

☐ Zombie parent

☐ Zombie child

☐ Someone screaming at child or significant other

☐ Tropical Zoom background

☐ Contraband

☐ Someone forgets to mute their mic and makes some remarks not meant to be heard by everyone

☐ Unfortunate camera angle creating effect of eight chins

☐ Someone working on a knitting or crochet project. (Spoiler alert: I am always that person.)

☐ Something that can be used as a murder weapon if you are trapped at a madcap dinner party, e.g. candlestick, wrench, or lead pipe

☐ Is that Sandra? What happened to her hair?

☐ Adult in pajamas

☐ Group chat being used to antagonize the moderator

☐ Silent laughing fit

☐ Someone with a bewildered, panicked expression as they struggle with technology

☐ A teacher searching job listings for scuba diving instructor in Hawaii

☐ Booze

☐ Nunchucks

☐

☐ Someone using camera as a mirror to see if they have any new wrinkles or pimples

☐ Someone who leaves the meeting ridiculously early on some false pretense (that's also always me)

And Now, We Rant

The art of ranting is older than civilization itself. Historical linguists agree that language was developed to express rage and exasperation when an early cave person stubbed his toe on a rock and shouted, "Gunnhhh gunnnhhh craaaa blug!" Those first noble words meant, "Gunnhhh gunnhhh rock toe!" The cave person repeatedly screamed "Gunnhhh gunnnhhh craaaa blug!" while hopping around the cave, stopping occasionally to throw the offending rock against the wall, and so, the world experienced its first rant. At least, that is what the historical linguists say.

The anthropologists say the historical linguists are a bunch of self-absorbed idiots, and the world's first rant occurred long before the advent of language, when one chimpanzee stole another chimpanzee's onion. The wronged party jumped around screaming and hurling feces at the other chimps and *that* was the first rant (stupid historical linguists).

Although I hate to take sides, I have to agree with the anthropologists. Have you ever been to the zoo? What's your favorite animal? I love the meerkats. Oh, sorry, I wandered into a tangent there. Where was I? Ranting, right! Ranting is incredibly cathartic, especially if you have any pent up emotions. It is the national sport in several smaller Oceanic nations and is being considered by the International Olympic Committee for the Summer and Winter Games. The summer heat incites particularly virulent rants, but winter rants are very exciting if the athletes combine their rants with the ski jump. Blimey, I went off on another tangent. Ranting. You. Let me wrap this up before I get distracted by another shiny tangent: if your child is participating in any level of distance learning, then I can assure you, you have some pent up emotions AND YOU NEED TO RANT.

Some things to keep in mind while preparing your rant:

1. Obscenities are necessary.
2. Grammar is optional.
3. If you get stuck, channel your inner Miss Piggy.
4. Or if you hate The Muppets (monster!), you can channel Galadriel when Frodo offers her the One Ring.

Turn the page, and I'll demonstrate a distance learning rant. Then, it's your turn!

Courtney's Distance Learning Rant

What, and I cannot empathize this enough, THE FUCK? I was told THREE WEEKS. THREE. FLIPPING. WEEKS. And Sweet Jesus, that included a week of spring break! So really, we were talking about two weeks without school and even that seemed outrageous. And now what has it been? SEVEN MONTHS??? ARE YOU KIDDING ME?

And there's literally no finish line in sight. The Superintendent just emailed that school will not start before January 11, 2021. Well blow me down and call me Papa Smurf. You know what "not before January 11" means? It means "Not until January 11 but we hate parents so maybe it will probably be a lot longer than that, heck, maybe we will do distance learning forever!"

I am barely holding on to my last shred of sanity here, and I'm not sure that shred can even be called "sanity." It more closely resembles a piece of petrified guano at this point.

⚠️ ⚠️ **CENSORED** ⚠️ ⚠️

GAY KOCKEN OFFEN YOM! ☆

Excuse me, I'm going to go destroy my last shred of sanity with Common Core math.

☆ This phrase was often used by Laurie, one of my two best friends in junior high. I thought it was hilarious at the time. I still do.

☆ Yiddish for "Go shit in the ocean!" Let me tell you, when you are the only kid at Catholic school with a Jewish mom, you get to impress the hell out of your friends when you teach them how to swear in Yiddish. In the seventh grade, our religion teacher loved to use the word "schmuck." Did you know that "schmuck" is Yiddish for "penis"? It is. I taught my friends this as well, and after that, it was very, very difficult to keep a straight face in religion class.

Now it's your turn! Show no mercy! And please, feel free to blatantly steal from my rant. I find the phrase "gay koken offen yom" to be particularly therapeutic.

Multiple Choice

Bubble in the correct response. Your answers will be graded by a soulless robot machine so if you do not fill in the bubble perfectly, your answer will be WRONG and you will have flashbacks to the special agony that is standardized testing. Which is a much better agony than distance learning, so there's that.

1. Distance learning is:

   (a) The neverending dark night of my soul.

   (b) Slightly more bearable than the apocalypse.

   (c) I'm sorry, has the test already started?

   (d) The reason I cry myself to sleep every night.

2. Since my child started distance learning, I have:

   (a) Cheerfully accepted this fun new challenge.

   (b) Questioned the meaning of life.

   (c) Starting occasionally barking like a dog.

   (d) Seriously considered joining the circus.

3. My mental health is:

   (a) Teetering on the brink of disaster.

   (b) Shredded beyond recognition.

   (c) Woefully propped up by ice cream and denial.

   (d) All of the above.

4. A train leaves Chicago at 4 o'clock:

(a) If this is Common Core math, I'm going to lose my mind.

(b) It's 4 o'clock? Hallelujah, it's happy hour!

(c) The train will never reach Florida because it gets attacked by zombies somewhere around the Cumberland Gap.

(d) How can I get on that train? I don't care where it is going, I just need to get away from this torture.

5. This activity book is:

(a) Quite possibly the only good thing to come out of distance learning.

(b) Worthless, but I will save it in case there is another toilet paper shortage.

(c) Better than Zoloft.

(d) The product of an idle mind in league with Satan.

6. The persons who organized my child's distance learning program are:

(a) National treasures.

(b) Our Robot Overlords.

(c) A bane to my sanity.

(d) Stupid.

7. Today's date is:

(a) Do calendars still work?

(b) The first day of the rest of distance learning!

(c) The Rapture.

(d) November 5, 1955.

8. At least once a week, I:

(a) Scream and start to speak in tongues.

(b) Eat literally all the sugar within a ten mile radius of my mouth.

(c) Wonder what part of this ordeal would have broken my parents' spirits.

(d) All of the above, bitches. All of the above.

9. If this continues much longer, I may have to:

(a) Join the Witness Protection Program.

(b) Have my memories of distance learning completely erased from my consciousness. Money is no object.

(c) Accidentally drop my child's laptop/tablet in the Grand Canyon.

(d) My brain cannot even begin to process the implications of this question.

10. On the first day back at real school, I don't mean hybrid, I mean "five days a week, full day, no masks," on that first day back, I will:

(a) Run across the playground like I'm the star of a new Broadway musical.

(b) See my therapist, get a facial, buy something stupid, and burn at least half of the toys that have destroyed my home.

(c) Go home, turn off all the lights, curl up in my bed in the fetal position, and alternate between hysterical laughter and ugly crying.

(d) I object to this question. It is making me feel uncomfortable flashes of hope and longing.

11. When I finish this test, I will:

(a) Return to plotting my overthrow of distance learning.

(b) Finish this glass of wine and pour myself another.

(c) Continue on to the next activity! So I can keep ignoring my kids!

(d) Finally go investigate why the kids suddenly got really, really quiet.

12. If anyone asks, I:

(a) Am supplementing my child's education with science experiments and art projects I sourced from Pinterest.

(b) Was nowhere near the school district's headquarters last Thursday.

(c) Am still haunted by the ending of *The Sopranos*.

(d) Have no idea how my child learned to swear in so many different languages.

Letter To My Future Self

Someday, this will be over. I know, I find that hard to believe myself. When this whole distance learning tragedy started, I could not imagine it lasting more than a few weeks. But now, we have been doing it for spring, summer, fall AND WINTER IS COMING. But this will end, I promise it will; and when it is over, we will actually forget the true extent of this experience. Enter: the letter to my future self. Let's start with an example from me.

DEAR FUTURE COURTNEY,

ARE THERE HOVERBOARDS YET? ARE OUR ROBOT OVERLORDS KIND AND COMPASSIONATE? NOW THAT THE DISTANCE ABOMINATION IS OVER, I WANT TO REMIND YOU OF SOMETHING VERY IMPORTANT: IT WAS AN ABSOLUTE UNMITIGATED NIGHTMARE. I KNOW YOU PRETTY WELL, AND I KNOW WHAT YOU ARE DOING. YOU ARE LOOKING BACK AT DISTANCE LEARNING AND THINKING, "HEY, THAT WAS NOT SO BAD. DISTANCE LEARNING ACTUALLY HELPED ME BECOME A BETTER PERSON!" YOU STUPID. FUCKING. IDIOT. DON'T YOU DARE GO ALL "LEMONS INTO LEMONADE" ON ME, YOU

OPTIMISTIC BITCH. THERE ARE NO LEMONS TO TURN INTO LEMONADE, OKAY? ALL THERE IS CRAP. CRAP CRAP CRAP. I DON'T CARE HOW MUCH VODKA YOU HAVE, CRAP IS CRAP. I AM SUFFERING. YOU GET TO DROP THE KIDS OFF AT SCHOOL AND THEN DO YOGA AND AFTER YOGA, YOU COME HOME TO A QUIET HOUSE WHILE I AM JUST BARELY SURVIVING. DO NOT, I REPEAT, DO NOT EVER, UNDER ANY CIRCUMSTANCES, ENTERTAIN THE POSSIBILITY OF HOME SCHOOLING PIPPA AND JULIAN. IT WILL DESTROY US. IF YOU HAVE TO CHOOSE BETWEEN DISTANCE LEARNING AND ANTARCTICA, CHOOSE THE PENGUINS. LOVE, ME

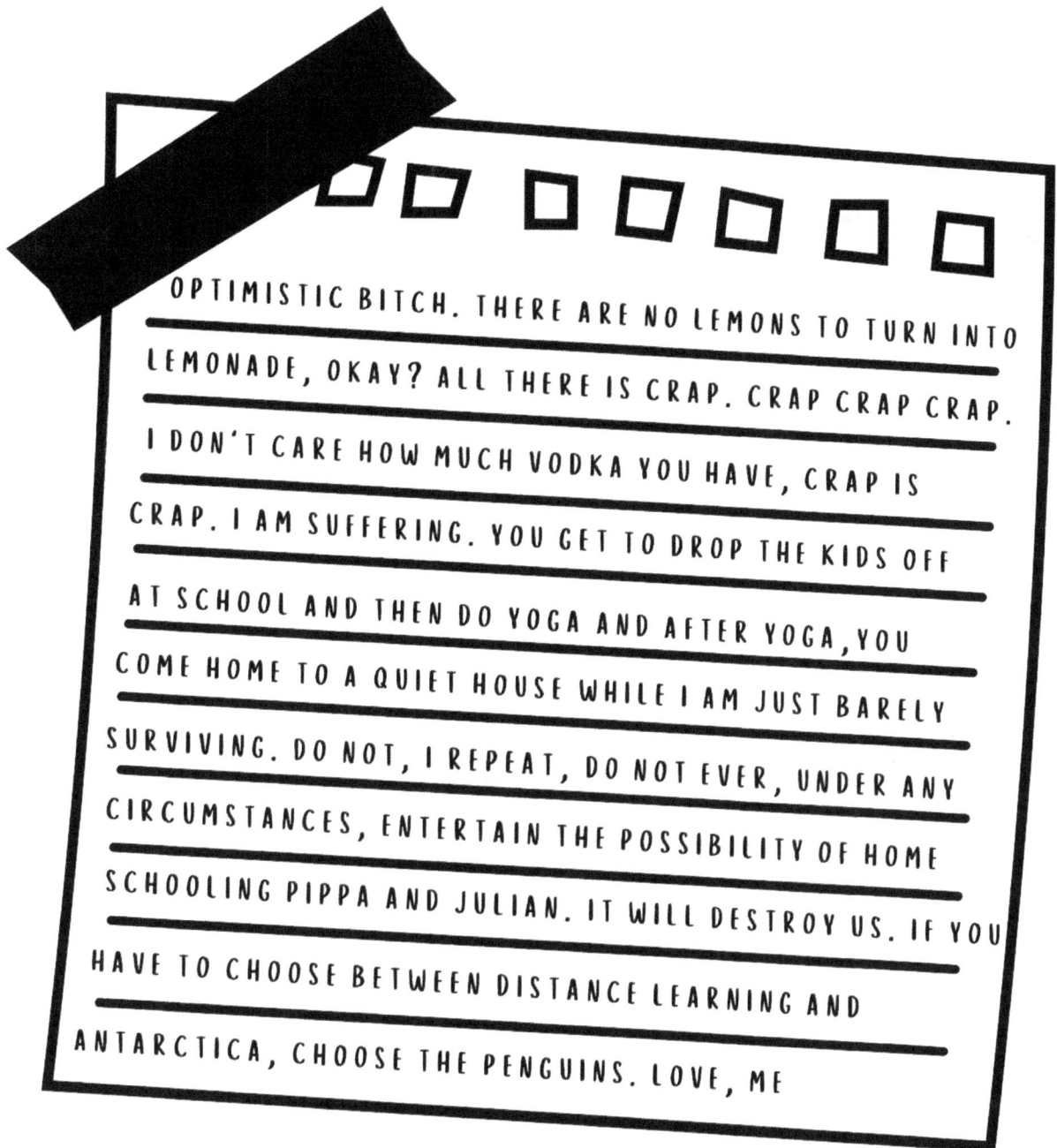

That felt even better than I thought it would! Now it is your turn to rip your future self a new asshole. Or bestow some thoughtful wisdom. But I highly recommend starting with the former before you get sentimental. Go on! Turn the page! Woot woot!

Yes, excellent. But more obscenities! More rage! Keep going! Don't hold back! Embrace the darkness! Your therapist does not need to see what you wrote. This is the therapy your therapist does not need to know about. Speaking of which, please, for the love of all things holy and sacred, no one tell *my* therapist about this activity book. I would like to be able to look her in the eyes when this is over.... (Just kidding, I'm totally sending her a copy of this book because I have the best therapist ever.)

Oh, wow, I can't believe you went that far. I'm feeling a little uncomfortable about that last bit. Those are some dark demons you are harboring. Maybe you should rip these pages out of the book, shred them into tiny pieces, burn those pieces, lock the ashes into a trunk, and drop everything into the Mariana Trench. I'm serious. The things you wrote ... that's the sort of thing that gets used against you in court. Destroy the evidence. But don't tell anyone I said so.

The Gentle Art of Calligraphy

Let us express our loftiest and most beautiful thoughts with the ancient art of calligraphy. With skillfully executed loops, we shall compose sonnets about the joy of distance learning. Oh, wait. Wrong book. (And if anyone writes that book, let me know. I have some hate mail I want to send.) In this book, we are using calligraphy to GIVE VENT TO OUR DARKEST THOUGHTS AND FEELINGS. Trace the sweet sentiments I have included below and then go pen some missives of your own.

Today I will not lose my mind in front of my child's class. I will get dressed and face the day with enthusiasm and joy. Barring that, I will at least suppress any homicidal urges I might experience during this long, long, oh so freaking long, dark night of the soul. How much longer must I wander this wretched endless hellscape? A month? A year? Two years?! How is this even possible?

Fuck shit piss and corruption, there are not obscenities enough in the English language to truly express the depths of my misery and relentless despair. Will we ever look back at this ordeal and laugh? I hope so, because that will mean I got my sense of humor back. You know what I want? A trophy. Something enormous and tacky that I can display for the rest of my life on the coffee table and if anyone gets their grubby fingerprints on my trophy, I will destroy them with my wrath. Or, if a trophy is too much to ask, I would at least like a feather boa. Amen.

Your Distance Learning Report Card

Here's a stupid idea: give this report card to your child or significant other and ask them to grade your performance during this historic abomination. Yeah, I'm not going to do that either. For the sake of your loved ones, just grade yourself. You can be brutally honest or utterly delusional. Choose your poison! Because no matter what grades you earn, distance learning still suuuuuuuuucks soooooo muuuuuuuuuuch.

Parent Name: _____

Children in Grades: _____

Explanation of Grades

A - An actual saint   D - Maybe a little too human
B - Superhero   F - No longer human
C - Very, very human   FF - Godzilla

Punctuality	_____	Perspective	_____
Patience	_____	Digestion	_____
Sense of Humor	_____	Ability to Numb	_____
Math	_____	Ability to Care	_____
Remembering to Feed Children	_____	Going Outside	_____
Appropriate Emotional Outlets	_____	Can You See the Floor?	_____
Organization	_____	Social Interactions	_____
Wardrobe	_____	Boundaries with Children	_____
Maintaining Social Alliances	_____	Ability to Cope With the	
Morale	_____	Relentless Sense of Doom	_____

THE END ☆

☆ I want to be clear. This is The End of *The Distance Learning Activity Book For Parents Just Barely Holding On To Their Last Shred Of Sanity*. It is not The End of distance learning. Hopefully, by the time you finish this activity book, the nightmare that is distance learning will in fact be over and we can all go dance in the streets. (I'm thinking a big choreographed number that involves some *West Side Story* finger snaps.) Wherever you are, whoever you are, I hope you are near the end of distance learning. And if not, I hope this activity book helped you get a firmer grip on your last shred of sanity.

And now, it is time for my:

PATHETIC PLEA FOR REVIEWS!!!

Please, please, please, please, please with sugar on top, PLEASE leave a review on Amazon! Your review will help other parents languishing in the wasteland that is distance learning find this book.

It will also help me make money. I really like money.

If you think this book is an abomination against mankind: Please still leave a review! If I only get a bunch of 5 star reviews, it looks like I just nagged my friends and family into leaving reviews. I don't actually have that many friends, but strangers on Amazon don't know that. (Though they will probably figure that out by page 8.)

I know most of you don't want to take the time to write a review. You know why? BECAUSE MOST OF THE TIME, I AM TOO LAZY TO LEAVE A REVIEW AND I'M A WRITER. It's actually not even laziness. It's just that as soon as I try to write a review, I get self-conscious and my brain freezes. If I write too little, I feel like a jerk. If I write too much, I feel like a pretentious jerk. I love reading, I love writing, but I hate writing reviews.

But writing a review for this book is like a bonus activity, and that means you can ignore your children's distance learning issues for a few more minutes. And heaven knows, we need all the credible excuses we can find to do that.

THANK YOU!

Acknowledgements

I would like to acknowledge That Kid in my daughter's second grade class who always interrupts the other kids and refuses to mute his mic, so we get to hear his mother's phone conversations and my god, That Kid really pushes my buttons. Without That Kid, I would never have reached my breaking point and if I had never reached my breaking point, I would never have been inspired to make this book. Thanks, That Kid.

My children, Pippa and Julian, for being excellent troopers during this never-ending soul-draining nonsense. I am so lucky to be your mom.

Kalea and Michelle - our text messages have been essential to my mental health during this crucible. If you ever stop texting me, I will go to your house and stare creepily through a window until you start humoring me again.

John V.- (Heads up folks, I am about to depart from my usual sarcasm and actually be sincere for a moment.) Thank you for your patience, sense of humor, flexibility, and compassion during distance learning. In particular, thank you for understanding when I told you that the Lesson 7 math quiz was pushing me over the edge. I was having a dark day.

Ben and Anna, thank you for opening your home for our pod! Thank you, Ben, for always asking if I'd like a cup of coffee, and thank you, Anna, for never making me feel crazy when I go off on one of my rants. You are my heroes. Also, you have excellent taste in books and movies, and it is always nice to find my people.

Rosie! Oh, Rosie! Thank you, thank you, thank you, for supervising our pod and always being patient with the kids. How do you do it? Magic? Can you teach me? You are an absolute saint.

Katie and Stefani - everything about our friendship has uplifted my spirits during this miserable nightmare. I want to clone you and sell your clones to other moms who need friends, but wow, that would be weird. So weird. So wrong.

I would also like to acknowledge Caffeine Free Diet Coke because caffeine destroys me but I just can't do distance learning without soda.

More acknowledgments this way! ➜

My dude, Kelly - knowing how lousy distance learning is in Maine reduces my bitterness just a teeny tiny speck. Can we meet in Kansas when this is over?

Matt and Katherine - best siblings ever.

Mom and Dad - best parents ever. You let me bitch and moan about distance learning and do not reprimand me for cursing and you promised to watch the kids for two weeks when this is over so Nathan and I can go to Maui.

Sara - you are a truly bitching sister-in-law. In this case, "bitching" means "really awesome but also great at bitching about distance learning with me."

Emily - I can tell you my darkest thoughts about distance learning and know that I am not being judged. Or, if I am being judged, you are doing a really good job of keeping a straight face. Either way, thank you.

Julie - Where's my fork?

I would like to keep acknowledging friends and assorted relatives but if I keep going, I'll never stop, and I have to quiz Pippa on her spelling words. There will be more books. There will be more acknowledgements. Consider yourself warned.

But I would be remiss if I did not acknowledge that 2020 has been the most epic year of my life. And though 2020 has been a veritable rollercoaster, with endless ups and downs, whiplash and nausea, vertigo and back pain, and an impending sense of certain doom, 2020 has also blessed me with abundant opportunities for personal growth. (Yes, I went there. I hope you do not feel completely betrayed.) I am now at a place in my life where I can stop worrying about fitting in and embrace my glorious self. That self happens to enjoy making snarky activity books, and I think that is pretty cool. For that, 2020, I am grateful.

And finally, I would like to acknowledge my husband Nathan for making 2020 as bearable as possible. I'm sorry for leaving so many empty cups in our bedroom. Thank you for not saying "that's lame" or "have you completely lost your mind?" when I told you I was going to make an activity book about distance learning for parents just barely holding on to their last shred of sanity. You are amazing.

What the hell?
You're still here?

The book is OVER. I've got nothing else for you. Stop it. Don't give me those puppy dog eyes.

Look, I wanted to include more activity pages but I'm in the trenches here. Do you know how many times I get interrupted in the space of -- hang on, the sound just stopped working for no apparent reason on my daughter's laptop. Where was I? Is this nightmare over yet? WHY IS THIS HAPPENING? ARE WE BEYOND REDEMPTION?!

Okay, deep breaths, deep breaths. Before I freak out again, I wanted to tell you that I have a newsletter. If you want to stay in touch and be the first to know about my next activity book, or if you just want to bear witness to my insane ramblings, go to my website, CourtneyHenningNovak.com and click on Newsletter.

Or you can type in this super awkward address:
http://courtneyhenningnovak.com/index.php/newsletter/

Or, you can scan this fancy code, and you will go on a magical adventure that takes you straight to my newsletter signup. I am really proud of myself for figuring this out, so please, humor me and use the fancy code and then tell me how using the code was the highlight of your day. Which is not saying much because #distancelearning.

ABOUT THE AUTHOR

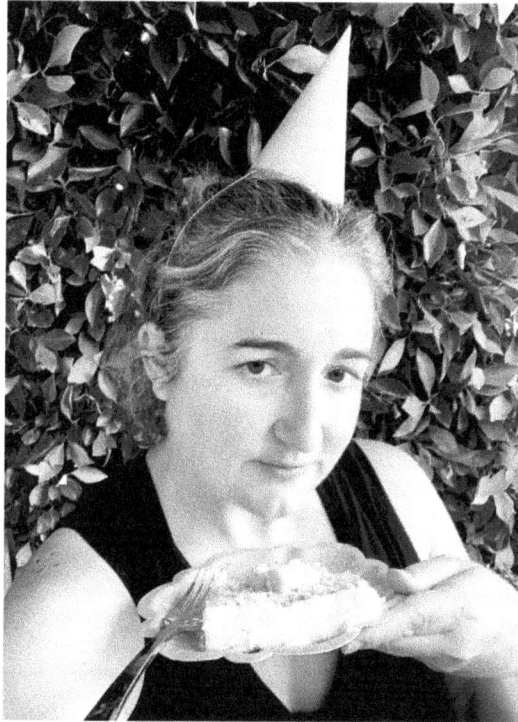

Extremely uncomfortable party hat.

I made you cake. Then I ate it. Sorry, not sorry.

Courtney Henning Novak is a mother just barely holding on to her last shred of sanity during the distance learning horror show. This is her second book. Her first book, *Adventures With Postpartum Depression: A Memoir*, does not have any activities. Not even Bingo. Courtney lives in Pasadena, California with her husband Nathan, their children Pippa and Julian, and a constantly fluctuating number of platies. (The platies have babies. Then they eat their babies, but a tenacious few manage to survive. At some point, a very large platy disappeared under mysterious circumstances. It's like the Discovery Channel in a ten gallon tank.) Courtney is the host of two podcasts, *Adventures With My Forties* (weekly, if distance learning behaves) and *Adventures With Postpartum Depression* (now mostly retired). If you are interested in more of her ramblings and tangents, visit her website, CourtneyHenningNovak.com or Instagram @Courtney.Novak. She is very lazy about Facebook so don't bother looking there. She thinks she once had a Twitter account but can't remember her handle. She is too old to figure out TikTok. Now that she has written one activity book, she intends to write many more. Then again, she might be leaving for Antartica next week. She hears the penguin schools are open for business.